Piano / Vocal / Guitar

ELTON JOHN/LEON RUSSELL/ ~~~~~ ON

Cover photo by Joseph Guay

ISBN 978-1-61780-332-1

HAL•LEONARD®
CORPORATION
7777 W. BLUEMOUND RD. P.O. BOX 13819 MILWAUKEE, WI 53213

Visit Hal Leonard Online at
www.halleonard.com

IF IT WASN'T FOR BAD

Words and Music by
LEON RUSSELL

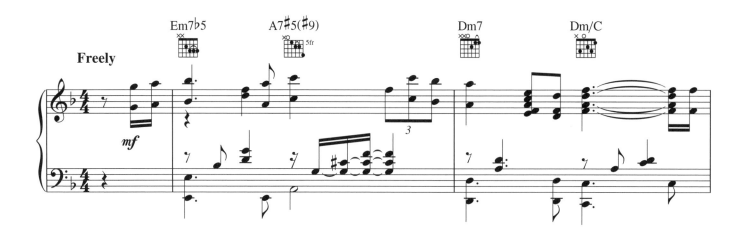

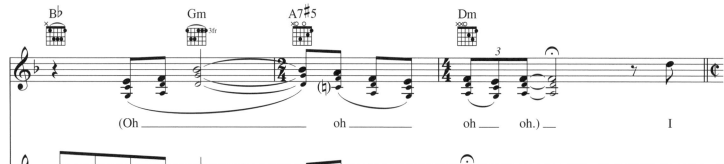

(Oh _____ oh _____ oh ___ oh.) ___ I

Laid-back, Funky Gospel

knew from the first night I met ___ you, some-thin' just was-n't quite ___

I on-ly saw __ what I want-ed to see. __

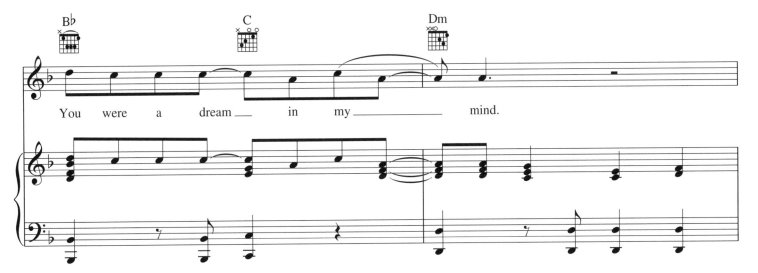

You were a dream __ in my _____ mind.

I'll nev-er know __ how you nev-er could be. __ It

did-n't take long for me to find. _____

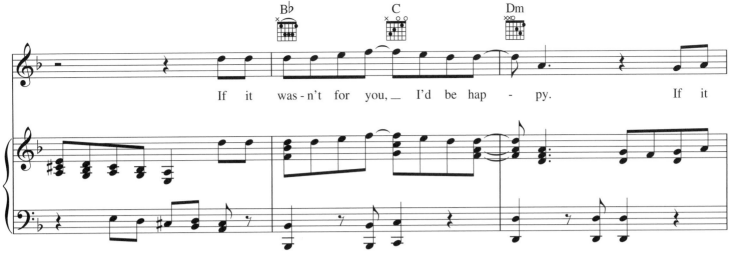

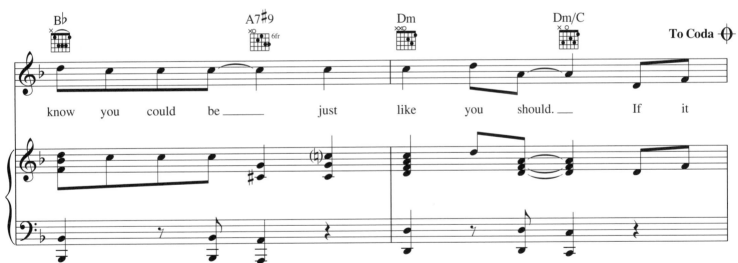

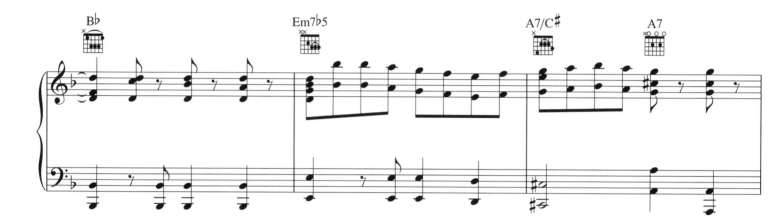

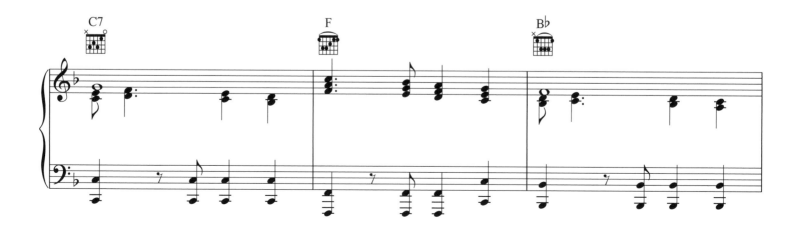

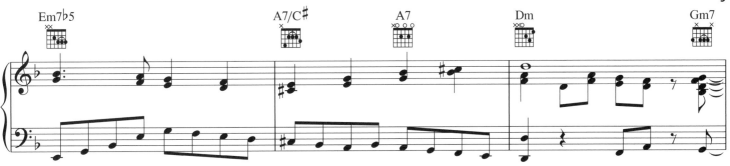

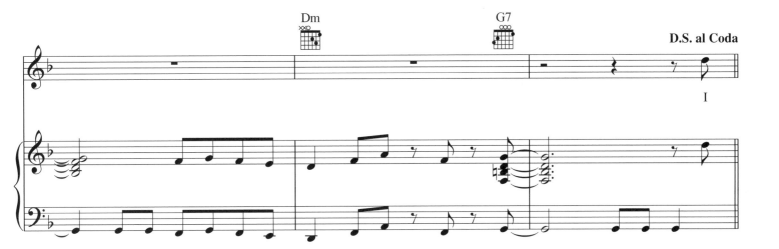

was-n't for bad, ___ you'd be good. ___

If it was-n't for bad, ___ you'd be good. ___

EIGHT HUNDRED DOLLAR SHOES

Words and Music by ELTON JOHN
and BERNIE TAUPIN

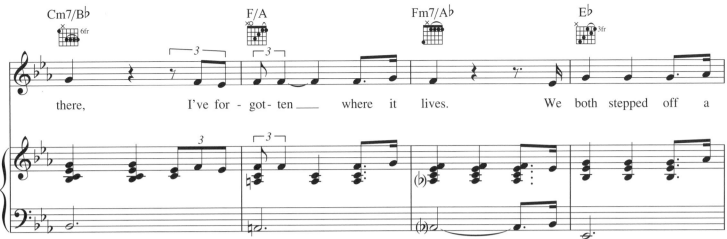

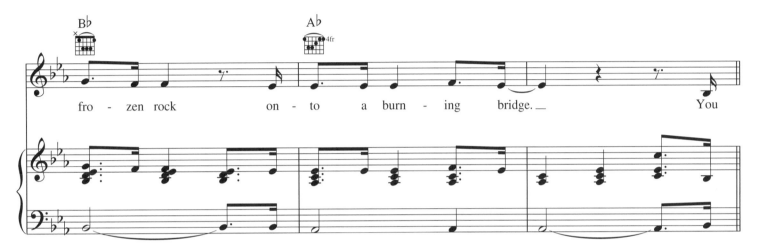

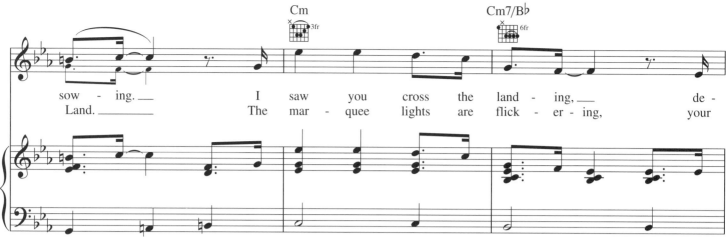

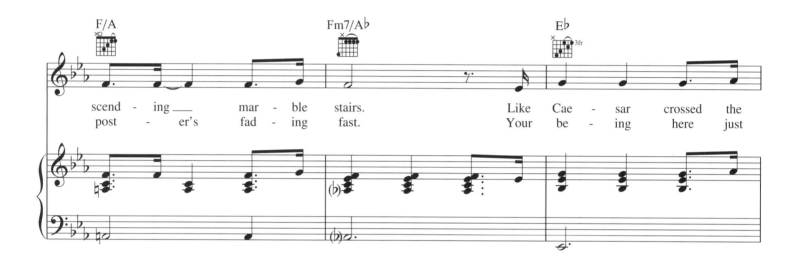

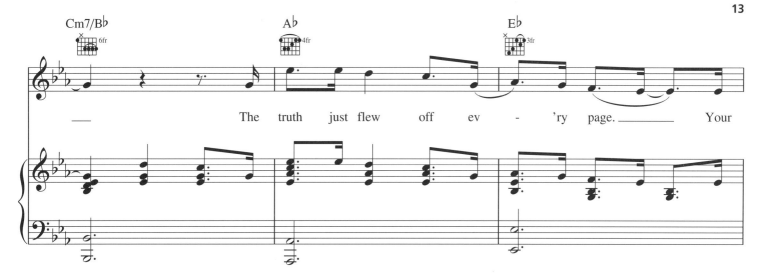

The truth just flew off ev - 'ry page. _____ Your

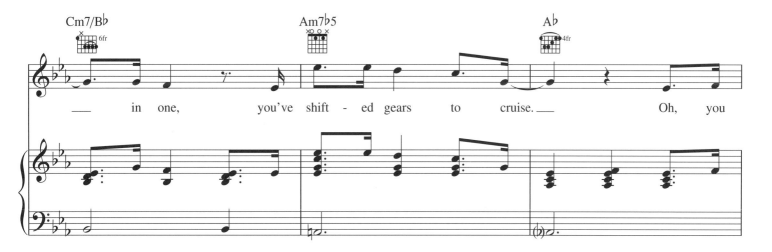

songs have all the hooks. _____ You're sev - en won - ders rolled __

__ in one, you've shift - ed gears to cruise. __ Oh, you

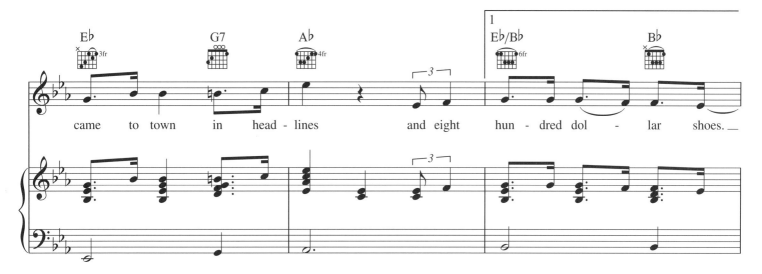

came to town in head - lines and eight hun - dred dol - lar shoes. __

14

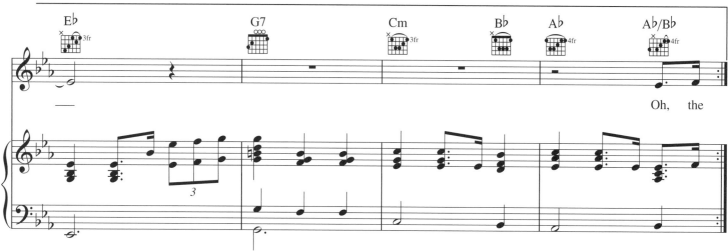

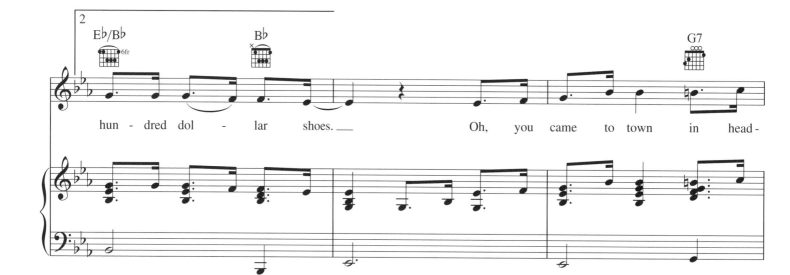

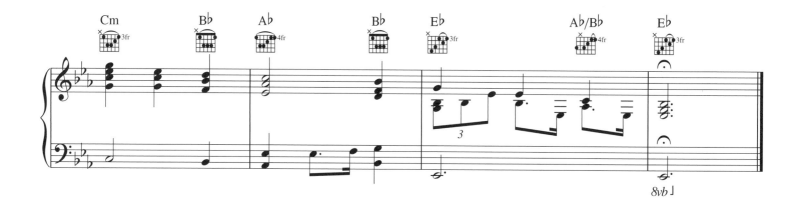

HEY AHAB

Words and Music by ELTON JOHN
and BERNIE TAUPIN

Funky Blues-Rock

It's a

con - stant strug - gle get - tin' up that hill. There's a change of guard ev - 'ry day.
crum - bling cit - y we were trapped for days, with a bro - ken sun a - bove the

clouds.
When you're cling - ing on - to a drift - wood boat, you pray a
Caught like Jo - nah for - ty fath - oms down, and a sign

great white whale _ might come your way. _
on the wall _ said, "Hope al - lowed." _

No free - way traf - fic in the
All the cryp - tic sym - bols carved

fro - zen North, just a chain _ link fence _ full of birds. _
on bone a far cry _ from a tat - tooed _ rose. _

And when the
And when the

har - poon's load - ed in the can - non bay, you'll be roll - in' through the pag - es lost for
boys in the rig - ging _ catch the wind, we'll all weigh an - chor, and it's west - ward _ ho. _

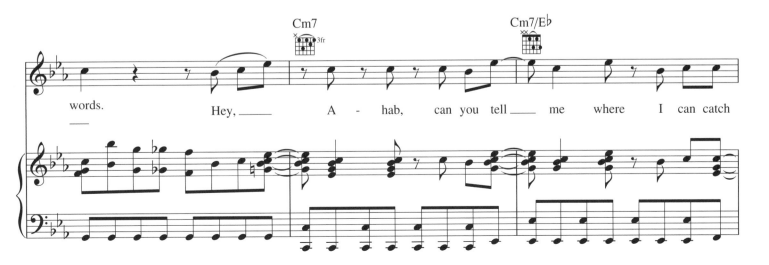

words.

Hey, _ A - hab, can you tell _ me where I can catch

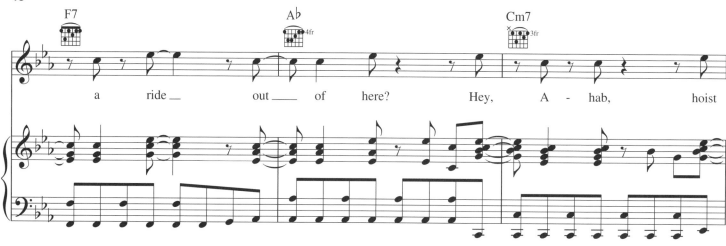

a ride ___ out ___ of here? Hey, A - hab, hoist

that sail. You got - ta stand up straight when you ride ___ that ___ whale. ___

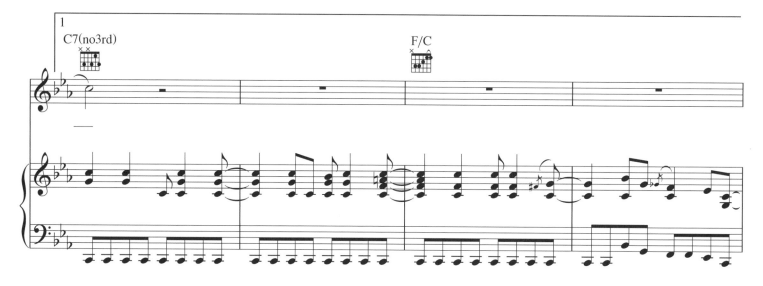

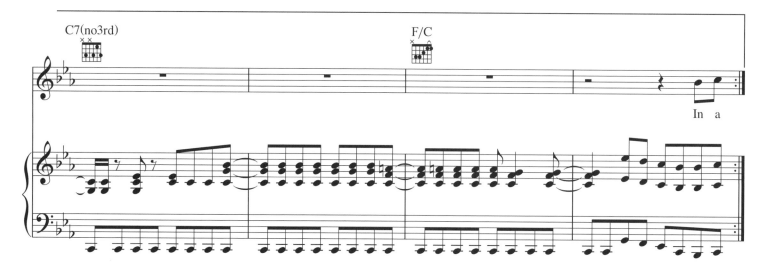

In a

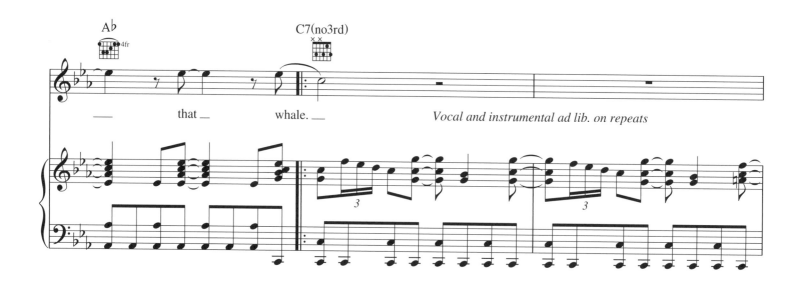

GONE TO SHILOH

Words and Music by ELTON JOHN
and BERNIE TAUPIN

Slow and Moody

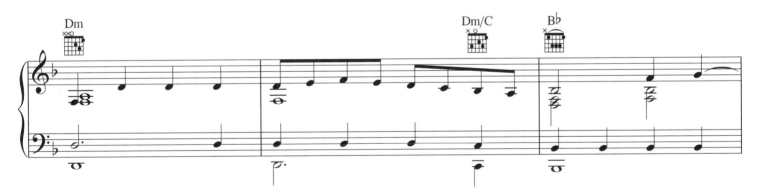

Luth - er left __ at first __ light Fri - day
old black roos - ter sang __ him down that

morn - ing. ___
dirt road. ___

Lit - tle Dan __ and Beck - y waved good -
His step seemed bold, __ his man - ner fan - cy

bye.
free.

They're gon - na have to share __ the weight __ to - geth - er.
I pray we see him a - live and well in the fall here

I - dle hands __ will see a good farm __ slow - ly die. __
than that God - for - sak - en place in ___ Ten - nes - see. __

Gone to Shi - loh ____ for the Un - ion. Shoul - der to

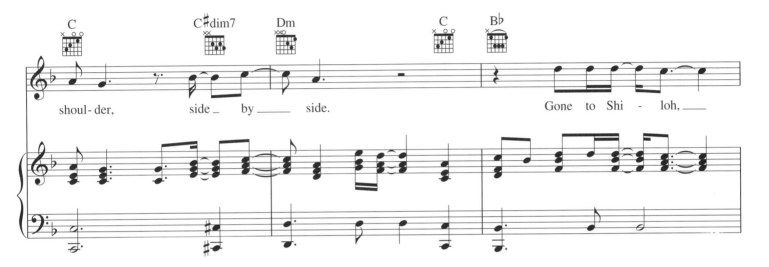

shoul - der, side _ by ____ side. Gone to Shi - loh, ____

{ hope springs e - ter - nal _____ when flags and bul - lets start to fly. __
men stand u - nit - ed _____ when flags and bul - lets start to fly. __

To Coda

A-pril's come, and the air smells fresh with rain. They

watched his sha-dow fade a-round the bend. He's head-ed

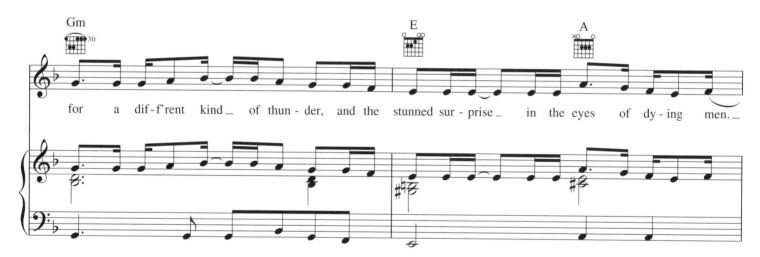

for a dif-f'rent kind of thun-der, and the stunned sur-prise in the eyes of dy-ing men.

Gone to Shi-loh for the

Un - ion.   Shoul-der to shoul-der,   side __ by _____ side.

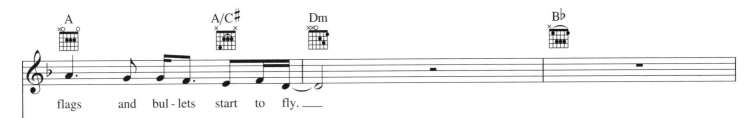

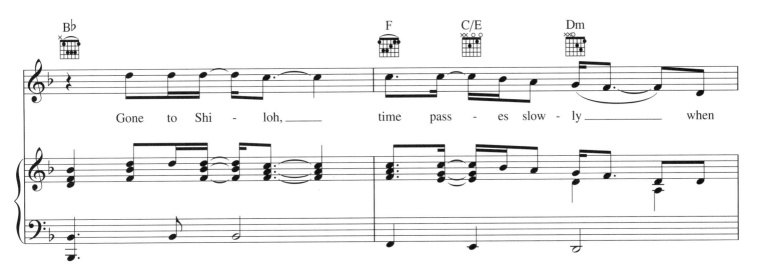

Gone to Shi - loh, _____ time pass - es slow-ly _____ when

flags   and bul-lets start to fly. ___

D. S. al Coda

The

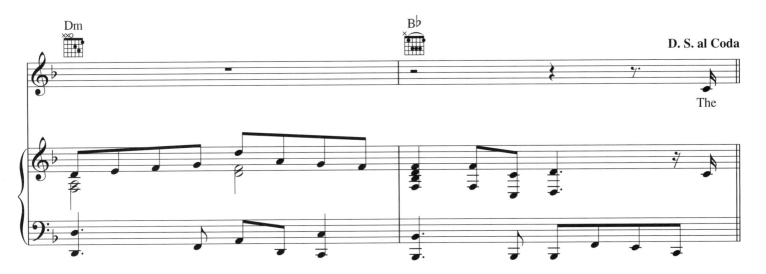

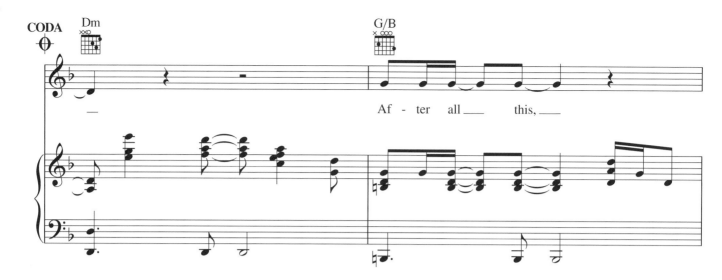

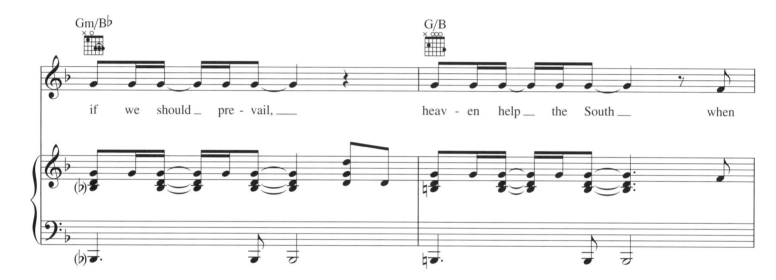

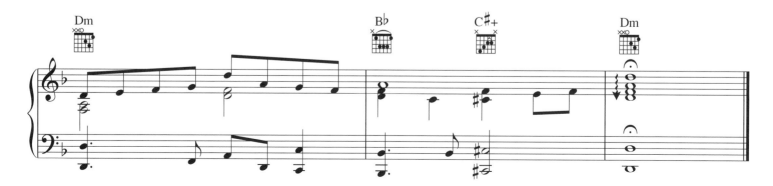

JIMMIE RODGERS' DREAM

Words and Music by ELTON JOHN,
BERNIE TAUPIN and T BONE BURNETT

Rolling Country groove

I'm look-in' at ___ a fu-

-n'ral wag-on roll-in' down ___ a

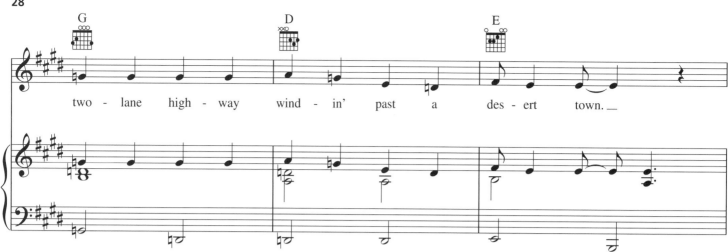

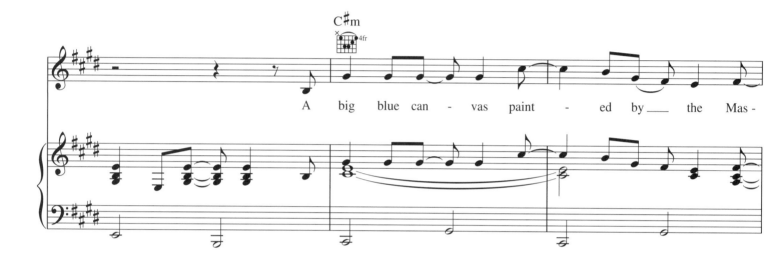

In that mir - ror, may - be that's _ what's left of me, _
dust - y, beat - en Del - ta boys _ cut - tin' heads. _

Instrumental solo

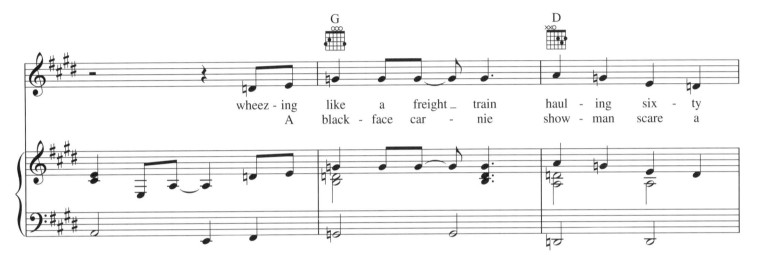

wheez - ing like a freight _ train haul - ing six - ty
A black - face car - nie show - man scare a

tons of steel. _ Air 'em out's _ the best _
song to death. _ In my short life, _ I've seen

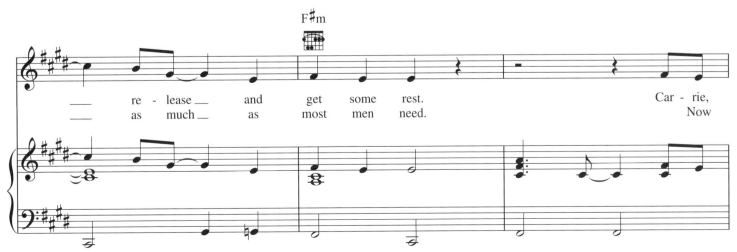

_ re - lease _ and get some rest. Car - rie,
_ as much _ as most men need. Now

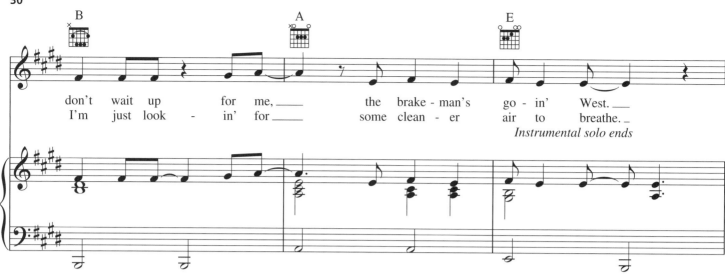

don't wait up for me, _____ the brake-man's go - in' West. ___
I'm just look - in' for _____ some clean - er air to breathe. _

Instrumental solo ends

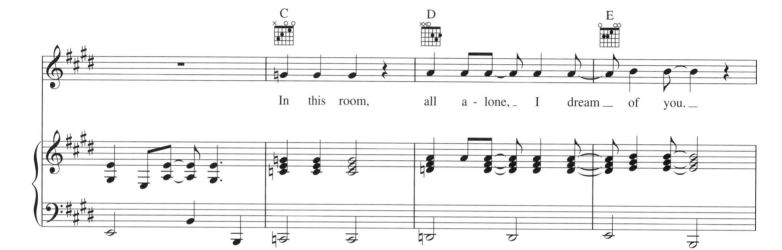

In this room, all a - lone, _ I dream _ of you. _

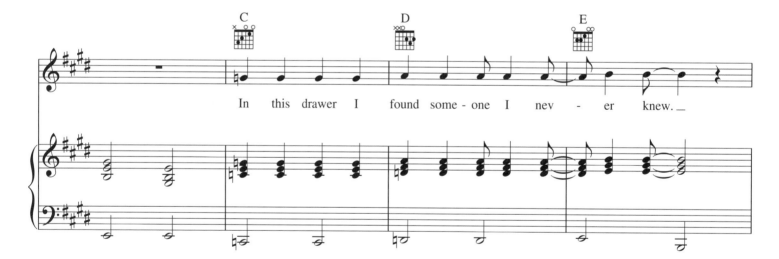

In this drawer I found some - one I nev - er knew. _

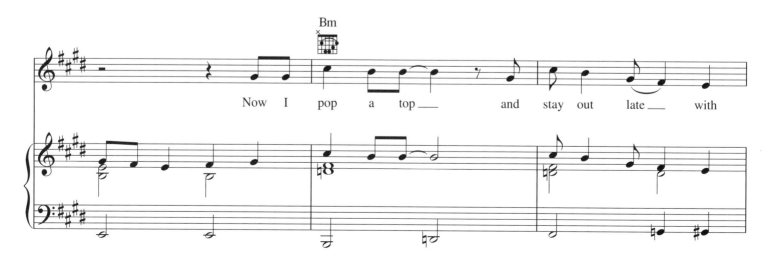

Now I pop a top ___ and stay out late ___ with

Gid - e - on. ___   Fall a - sleep to

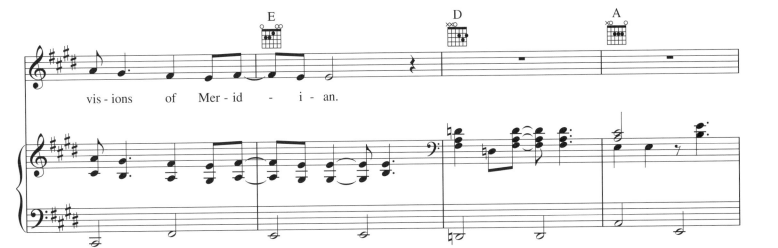

vis - ions of Mer - id - i - an.

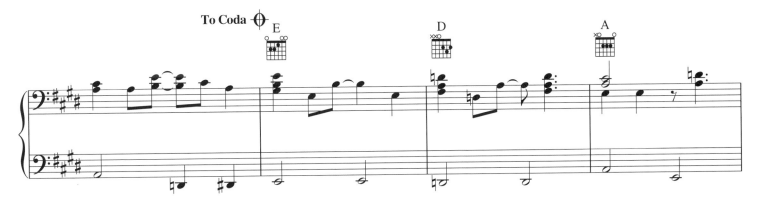

To Coda

I've seen   Far a - way, ___

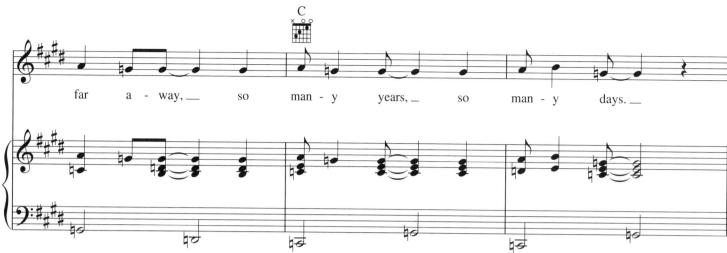

far a - way, __ so man - y years, __ so man - y days. __

All a - long __ this brok - en land __ I've seen a lov - er's emp -

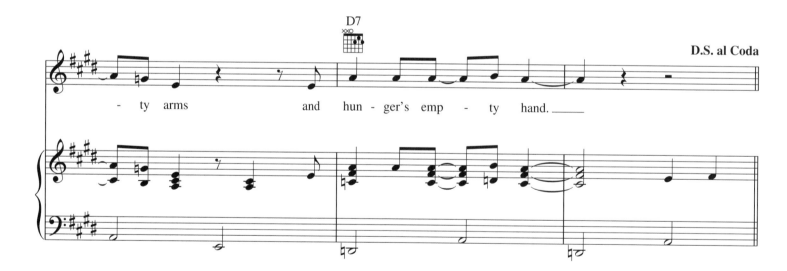

D.S. al Coda

- ty arms and hun - ger's emp - ty hand. ____

CODA

THERE'S NO TOMORROW

Words and Music by ELTON JOHN,
LEON RUSSELL, T BONE BURNETT
and JAMES TIMOTHY SHAW

side the next __ mo - ment, __ noth - ing __ might be. __
end up, no __ ques - tion, __ out - side of death's door.

__ The an - swer's not cer - tain, __ no
__ There's no eas - y an - swer __ to the

time to de - cide. __ Is this the last __
ques - tion at hand. __ So eas - y to __

cur - tain? __ There's no place to hide. __ }
ask, and not un - der - stand. __ }

There's no to-mor - row, ___

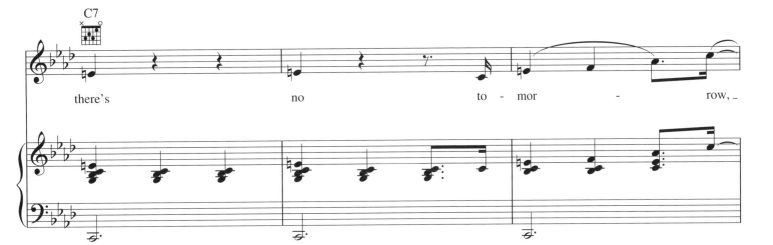

there's no to-mor - row, ___

there's ___ no to -

mor - row, ___ there's on -

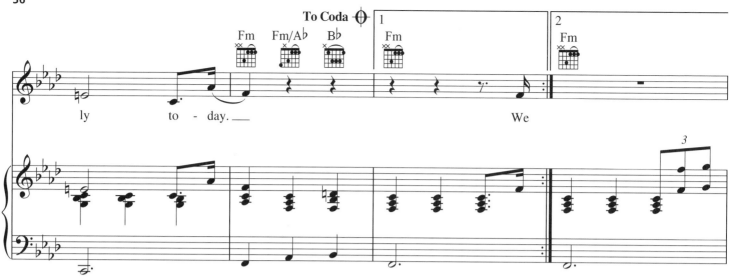

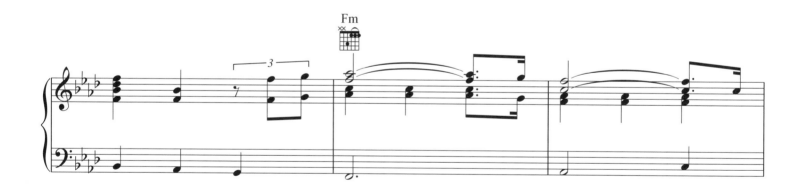

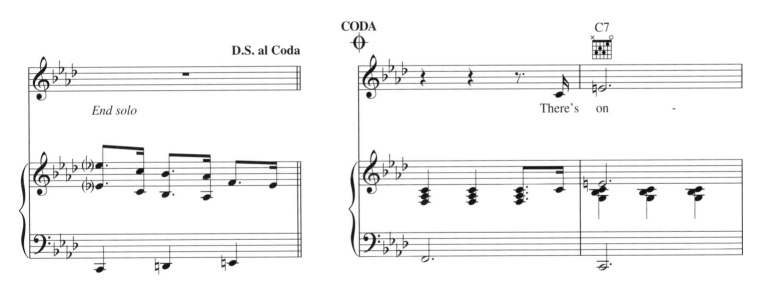

CODA

There's on -

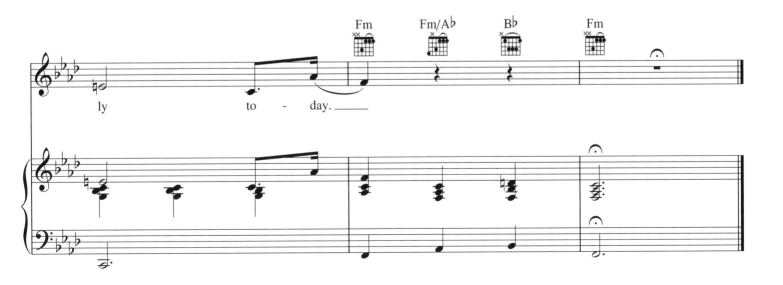

ly to - day.

MONKEY SUIT

Words and Music by ELTON JOHN
and BERNIE TAUPIN

Medium Honky-Tonk Rock

driv-in' south,   noth-in' left to   prove. __   You come back here   in your

cow-boy   boots, __   dressed to kill   in your mon-key   suit. __

Ev-'ry pose you strike,   ev'-ry frame they   shoot   shows you dressed

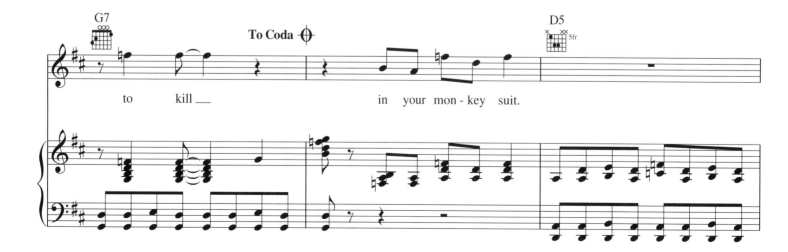

to   kill __   in   your mon-key   suit.

Build your lad -

Ooh, yeah. ___

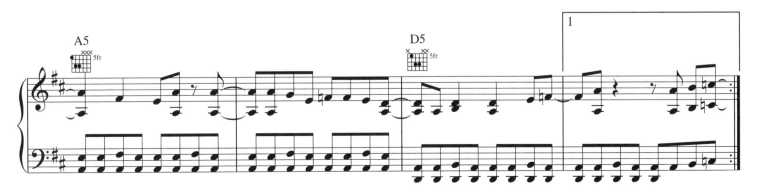

A5

D5

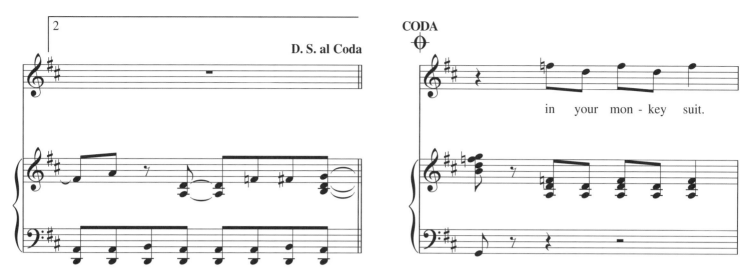

CODA

in your mon - key suit.

Oh, yeah. ___

Ev -'ry pose you strike, ev'-ry frame they shoot shows you dressed to kill ___

in your mon - key suit. Mon - key suit.

Mon - key suit.

Mon - key suit.

THE BEST PART OF THE DAY

Words and Music by ELTON JOHN
and BERNIE TAUPIN

Gentle Ballad

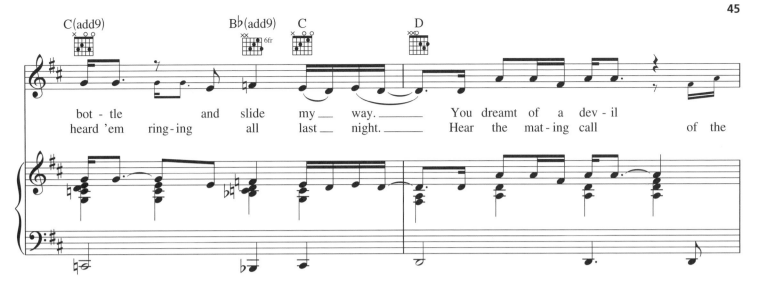

bot - tle   and slide   my   way. _____ You dreamt of a dev - il
heard 'em ring-ing   all   last __ night. _____ Hear the mat - ing call   of the

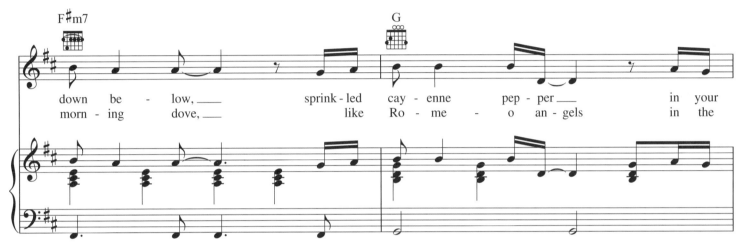

down be - low, ____ sprink - led cay - enne   pep - per _____ in your
morn - ing dove, ____ like Ro - me - o an - gels   in the

sug - ar bowl. __ But he's a fool,   and he's a thief. __ Got
roof a - bove. __ Rains will come,   sweet and clean. __ Let the

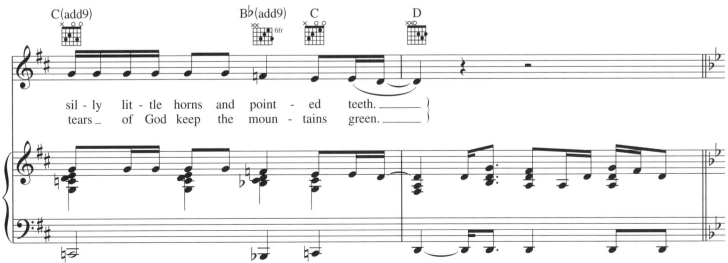

sil - ly lit - tle horns and point - ed teeth. _____
tears _ of God keep the moun - tains green. _____

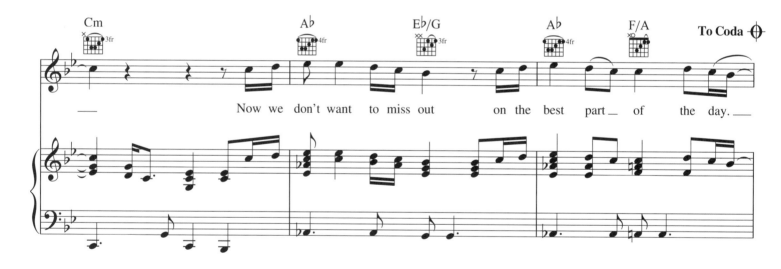

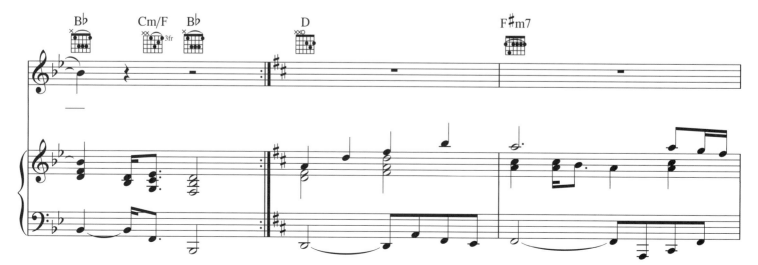

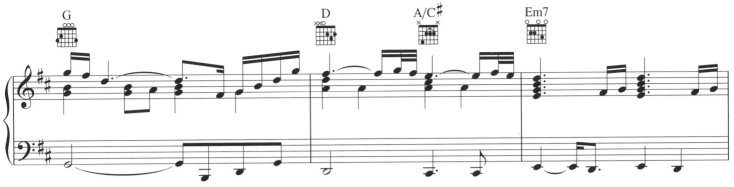

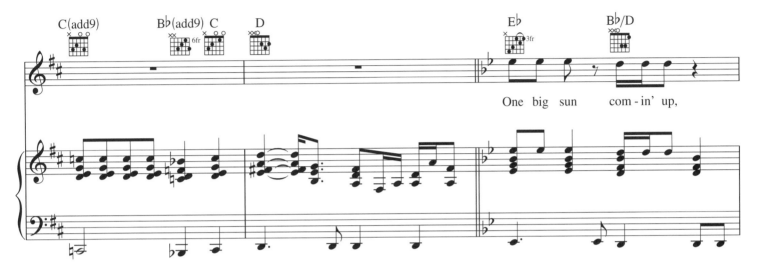

One big sun com-in' up,

old moon go-in' down. __ Thun-der break-ing in the east, __ I'm gon-na

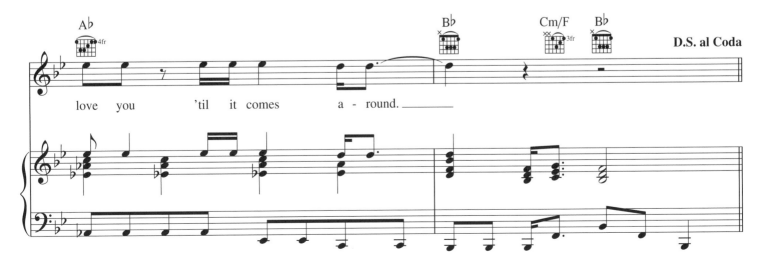

love you 'til it comes a - round. ____

D.S. al Coda

You're my best friend, you shared my cra-zy ways.

Now we don't want to miss out on the best part __ of the day. __

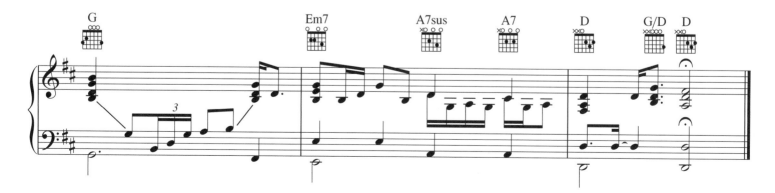

A DREAM COME TRUE

Words and Music by ELTON JOHN
and LEON RUSSELL

Bright Honky-Tonk Blues

all the things you __ do. ____ Now the

time has __ come, __ I know __ you're a dream come __ true. __

You make me so com - plete __ with the
feel the __ beat __ of the

things you __ do. ____ And the mu - sic's __ sweet, __ make me
danc - ing __ drums, __ and now I ____ know __ we're gon - na

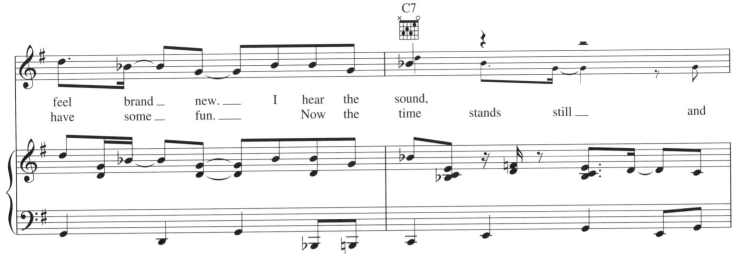

feel   brand __   new. __   I hear the   sound,
have   some __   fun. __   Now the   time   stands   still __   and

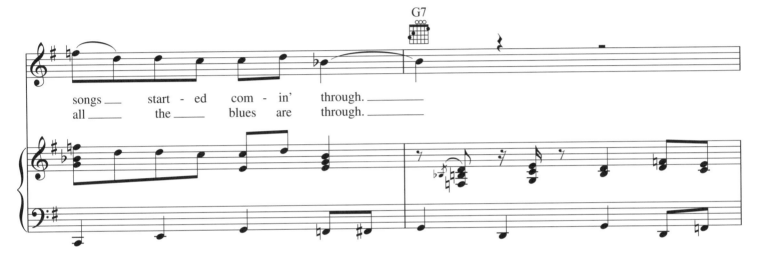

songs __   start - ed   com - in'   through. _____
all __   the __   blues   are   through. _____

Some-how   I   know   you're   a   dream   come   true. __
And   now   I   know __   what   I'm   gon - na   do. __

It   takes   my   breath __   when   it

sounds that ___ way. It seems like ___ you ___ can chase the

clouds a - way. ___ And I feel so ___ good ___ in each and

ev - 'ry ___ way, ___ and life is ___ good each and ev - 'ry day. ___ Now I

feel ___ the beat ___ of the danc - ing drums, ___ and ___ now I know we're gon - na

have _ some fun. _ Now the time stands still, _ and the blues are through. _

_ And now I know _

what _ I'm gon - na do. _____ Oh, _____ yeah.

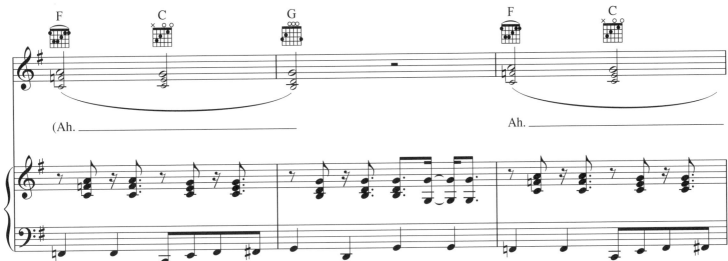

(Ah. _____ Ah. _____

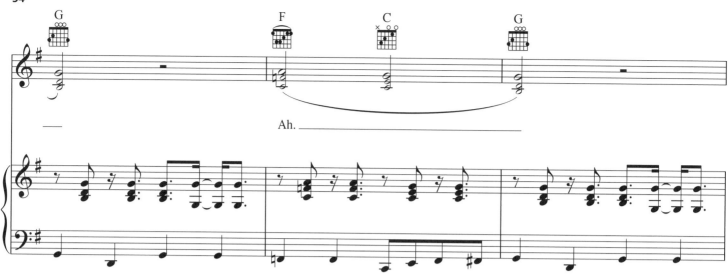

Ah.

Ah.) Now I

D. S. al Coda

CODA

ev - 'ry day.

(Doo,   doo,   doo.   Doo,   doo,   doo.)

Piano ad lib. on repeats

Repeat and Fade   **Optional Ending**

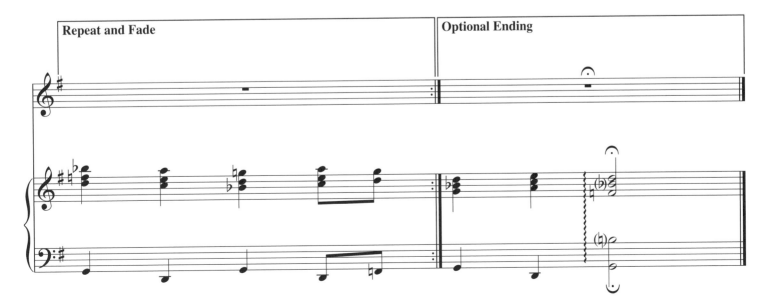

WHEN LOVE IS DYING

Words and Music by ELTON JOHN
and BERNIE TAUPIN

Slow Power Ballad

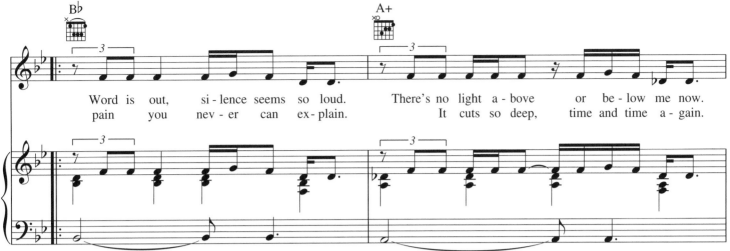

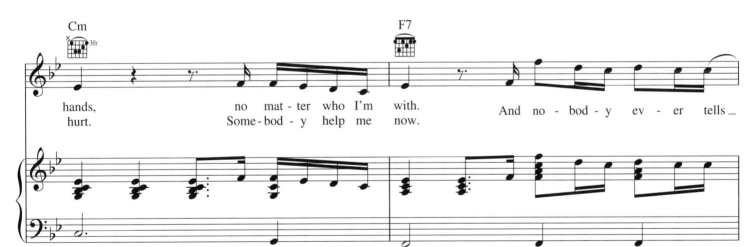

-ing, it just gets a lit-tle cold-er.___ And we stop try-ing, we stop

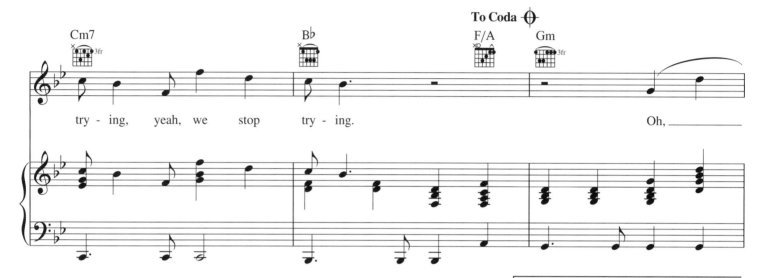

To Coda ⊕

try-ing, yeah, we stop try-ing. Oh,_____

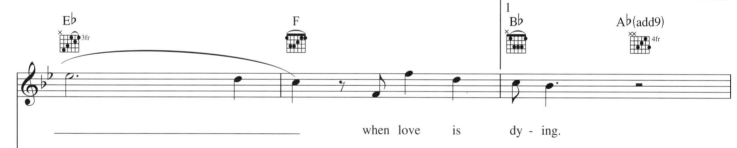

_____ when love is dy-ing.

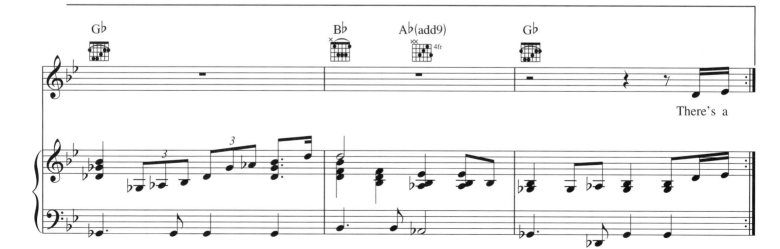

There's a

dy - ing. But

love nev - er gets to show _ you, and I nev - er got to know _ you. No, we

nev - er stood a chance _ when love was dy - ing. And

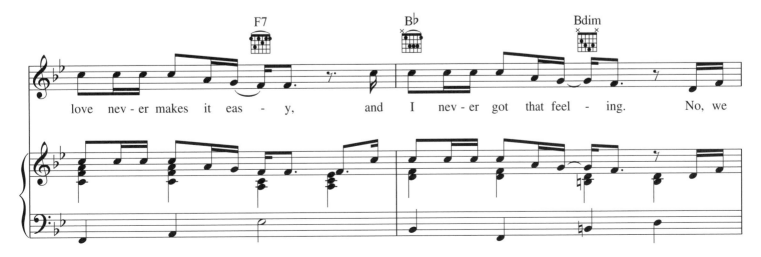

love nev - er makes it eas - y, and I nev - er got that feel - ing. No, we

D. S. al Coda

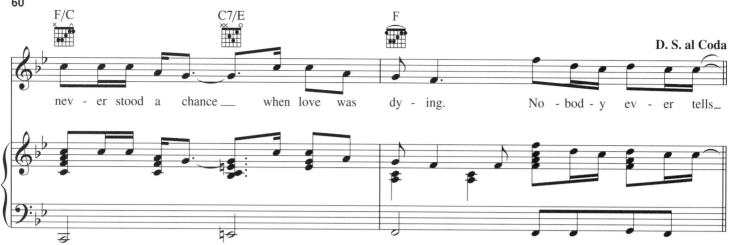

never stood a chance ___ when love was dy - ing. No - bod - y ev - er tells ___

CODA

Oh, _____ when love is

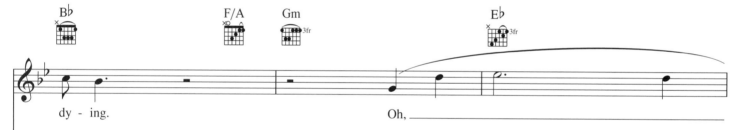

dy - ing. Oh, _____

___ when love is dy - ing. _____

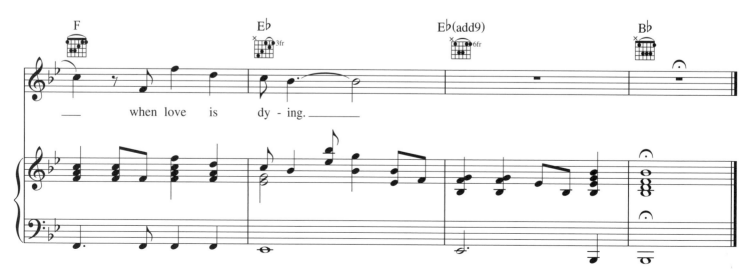

I SHOULD HAVE SENT ROSES

Words and Music by LEON RUSSELL
and BERNIE TAUPIN

what I felt all a - long the way. ____ Just

won - der - ing how come ____ I could - n't take your breath a - way.

'Cause I nev - er sent ros - es, ____ I nev - er did e - nough. ____

I did - n't know how to love _____ you, ____

though I loved you so much. _____

And I should have sent ros - es _____ when you crossed my

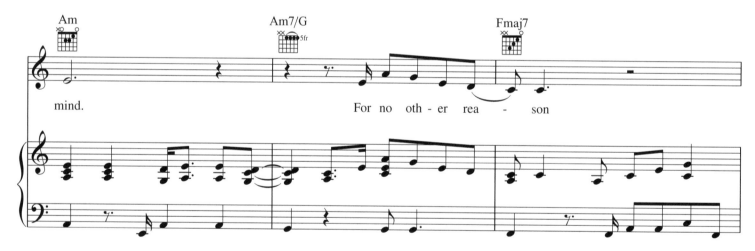

mind. For no oth - er rea - son

than the fact you were mine, _____ I should have sent ros -

es.

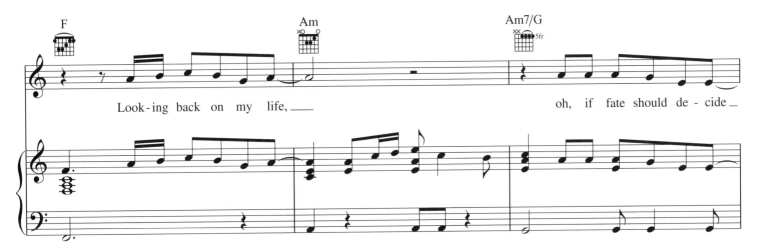

Look - ing back on my life, ___   oh, if fate should de - cide ___

I could do it all ov - er a - gain, ___

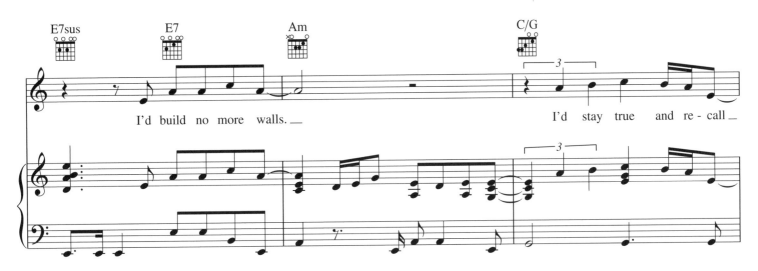

I'd build no more walls. ___   I'd stay true and re - call ___

the frag-rance of you on __ the wind. __

You'll get bet-ter than me, ____ some-one who can see __

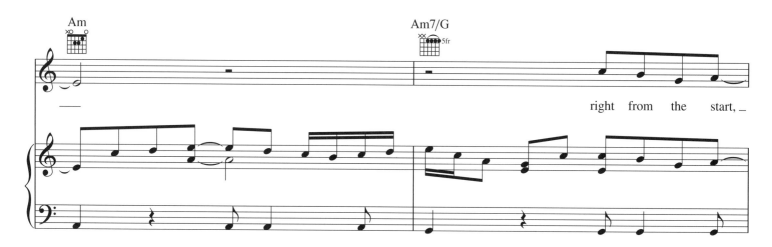

right from the start, __

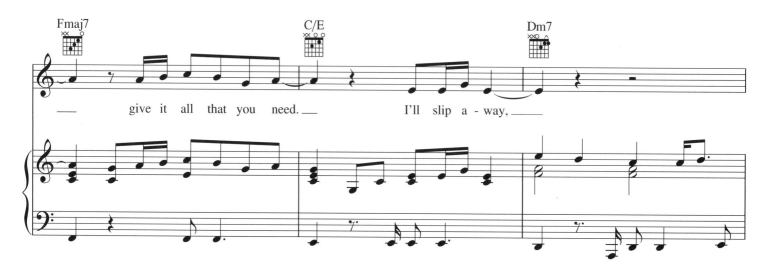

give it all that you need. __ I'll slip a-way, _____

'Cause I nev-er sent ros-

D. S. al Coda

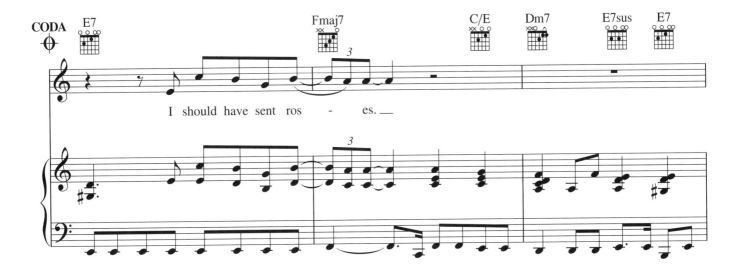

I should have sent ros - es. ___

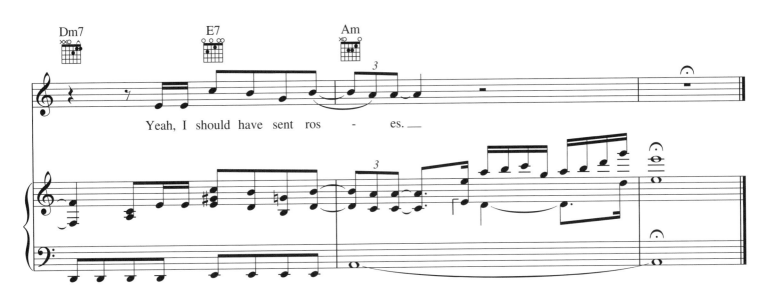

Yeah, I should have sent ros - es. ___

HEARTS HAVE TURNED TO STONE

Words and Music by
LEON RUSSELL

Bright Honky-Tonk Blues

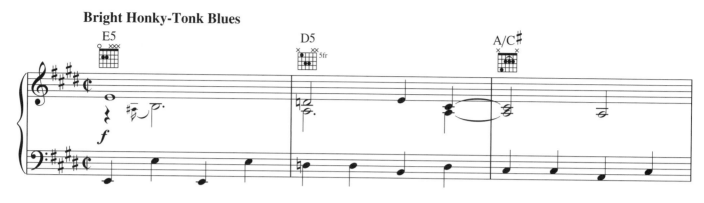

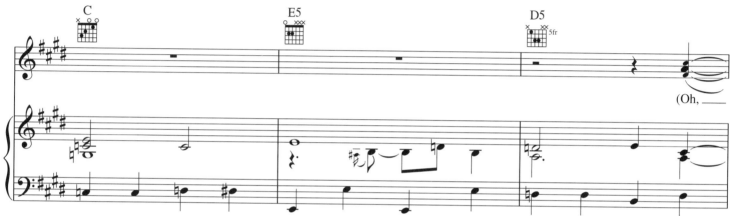

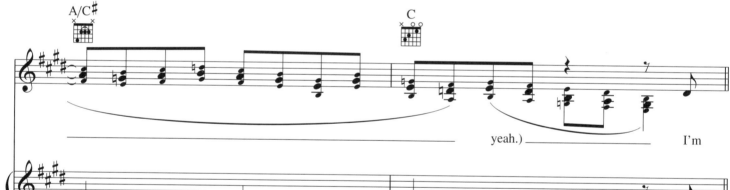

(Oh, _____ yeah.) _____ I'm

out here in ___ the dark - ness,   I hear the howl - ing wind.
Now the sun ___ is ris - ing   high - er in ___ the sky.

Some - times I sit and won - der, will I
The morn - ing light is crawl - ing from the

ev - er see love a - gain? ____
dark - ness of the night. ____
Look - ing for ____ an an -
Rain - drops keep ____ on fall -

swer, not an eas - y ____ thing ____ to find. ____
ing, there is no ____ light ____ of day. ____

____ (Oh, _____ yeah.) ____
____ (No background vocal on repeat)

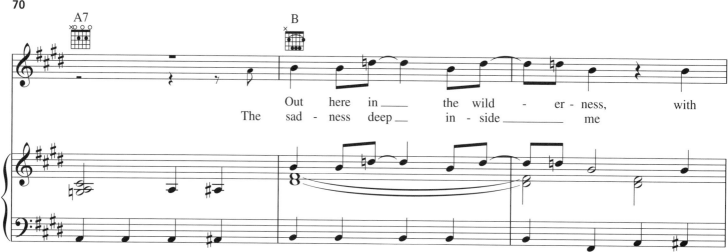

Out here in ____ the wild - er - ness, with
The sad - ness deep ____ in - side _____ me

ques - tions ____ on ____ my mind. _____
does - n't seem to go a - way. _____

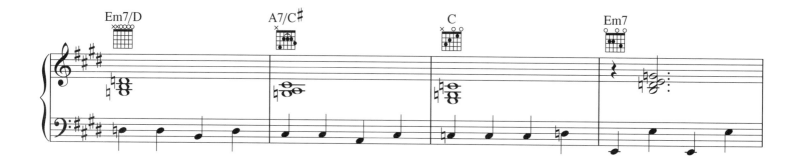

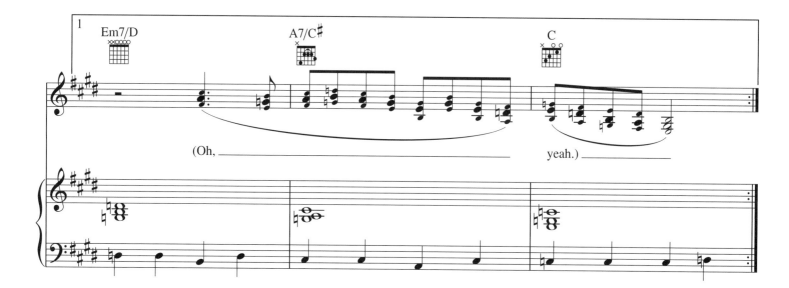

(Oh, _____ yeah.) _____

(Oh, _____ yeah.) _____ And there's

no way _ out, _____ no road _ home. _____ I'm

lost in _ doubt _____ and all a - lone. The

time has _ come _____ when love is _ done. _____ Our

hearts have fi - n'lly turned __ to stone. ___

No more bright to - mor - row, __ on - ly sad __ to - day. ___ My

heart is filled with sor - row. __ The pain won't go a - way. ___ I

try to keep __ from cry - ing all ____ night long and through the day. __

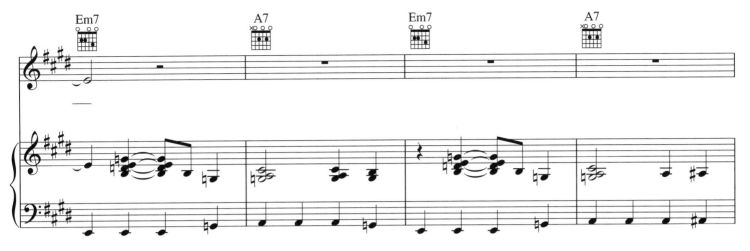

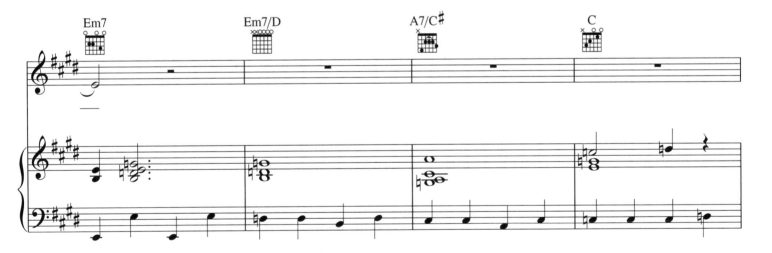

Lost and all ___ a - lone, ___ our hearts have fi - n'lly turned to ___ stone. ___

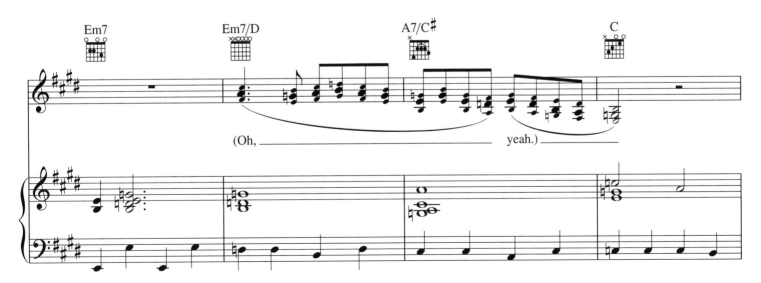

(Oh, _____ yeah.) _____

D.S. al Coda

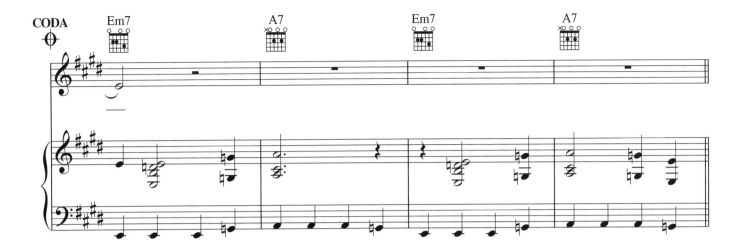

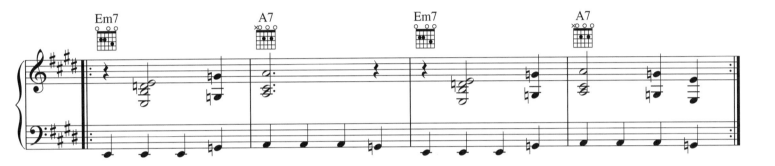

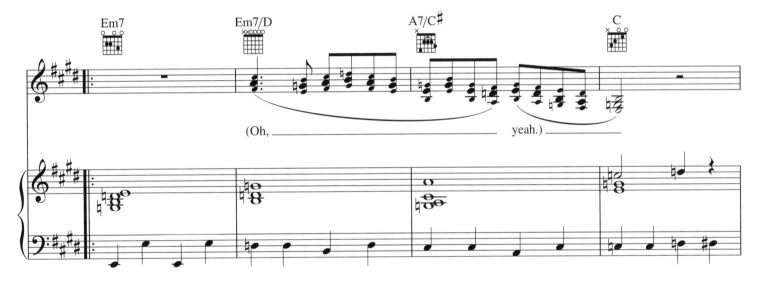

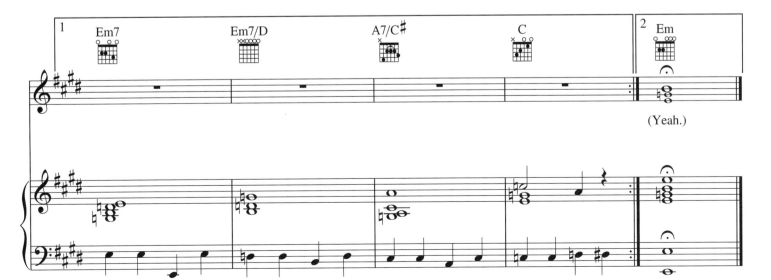

NEVER TOO OLD
(To Hold Somebody)

Words and Music by ELTON JOHN
and BERNIE TAUPIN

nev - er too old, nev - er too old to ___ hold some -

bod - y. Don't you know, you're nev - er too old,

nev - er too old to hold ___ some - bod - y. ___ You're

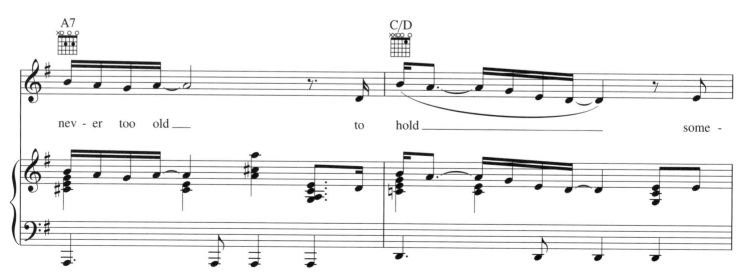

nev - er too old ___ to hold _____ some -

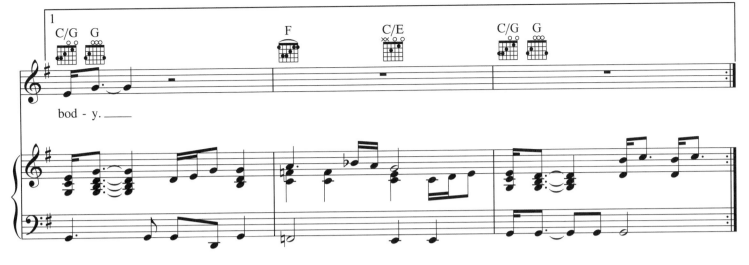

bod - y. ___

bod - y. ___ I could bet on a horse, ___ but I'm bet - ting on

you. You still got what it takes, ___ you got

noth - ing, noth - ing to prove. ___

You're nev - er too old,

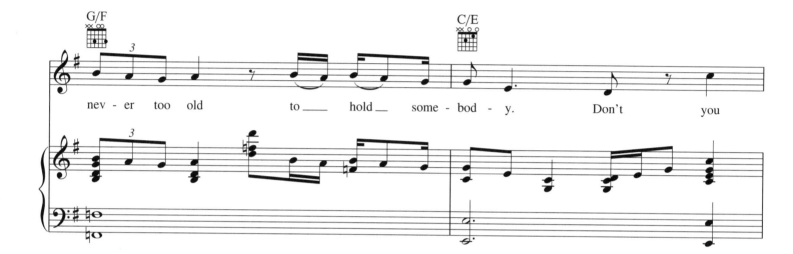

nev - er too old to ___ hold ___ some - bod - y. Don't you

know you're nev - er too old,

nev - er too old to hold ___ some - bod - y. ___ Oh, you're

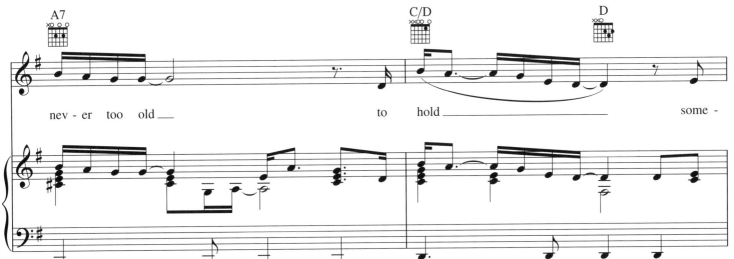

nev - er too old ____ to hold _____ some -

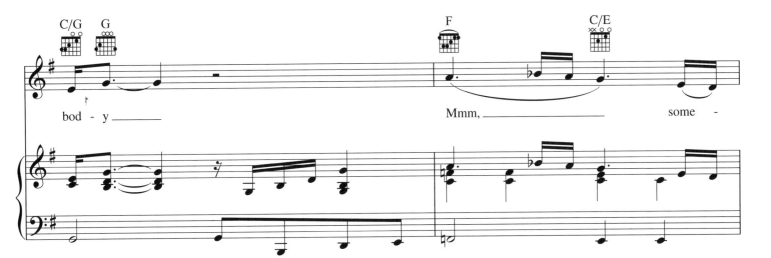

bod - y ____ Mmm, _____ some -

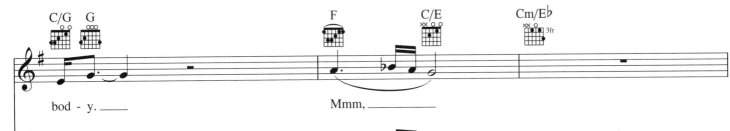

bod - y. ____ Mmm, _____

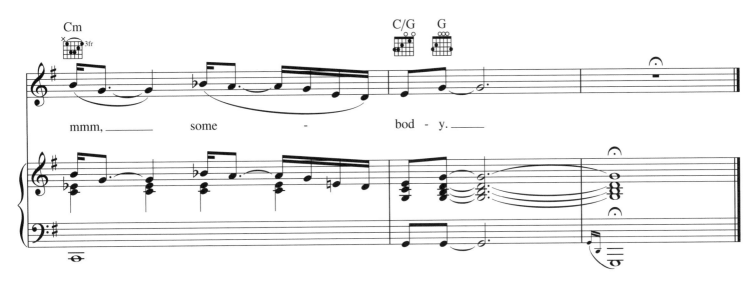

mmm, _____ some - bod - y. ____

IN THE HANDS OF ANGELS

Words and Music by
LEON RUSSELL

Gospel Hymn

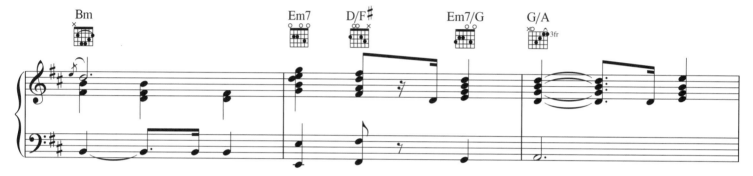

Well, I could have been
was _____ a

sick, I could have died. _____ I
whole new race _____ when

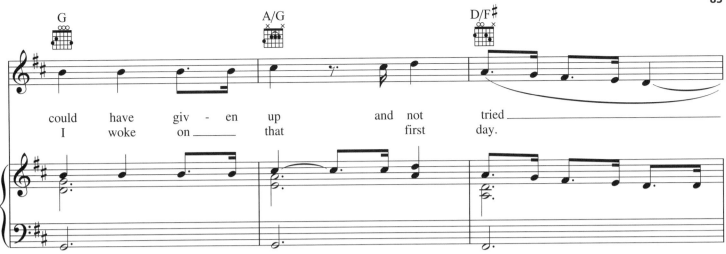

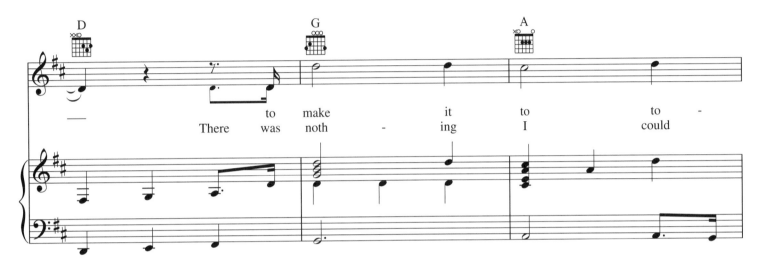

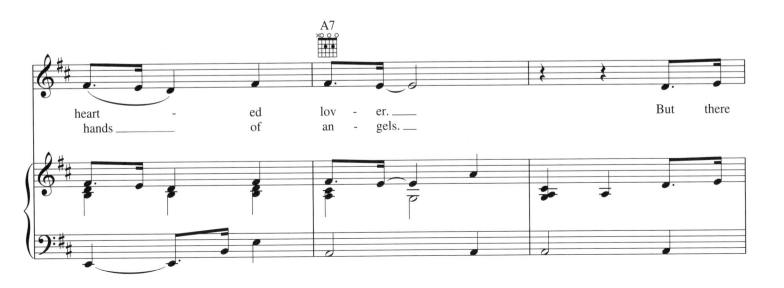

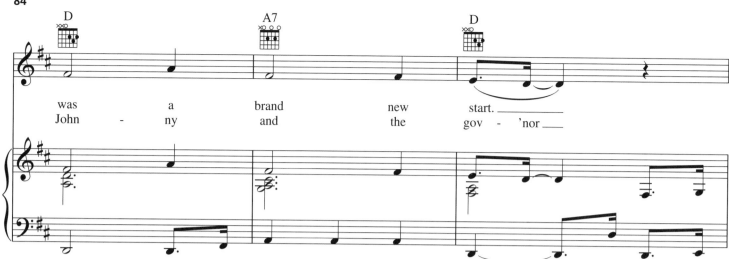

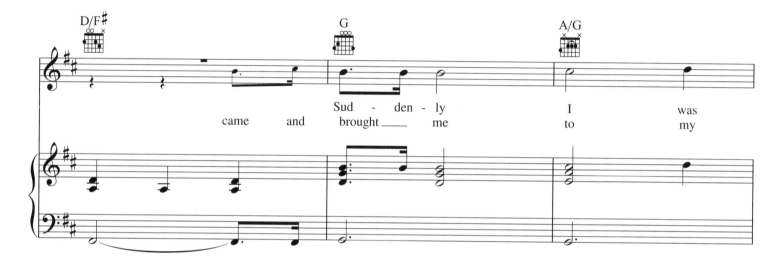

mu - sic   I _____ was   sing - in'. ___
lose   all   my _____ de - fense. _____

It

And they knew all ___ the

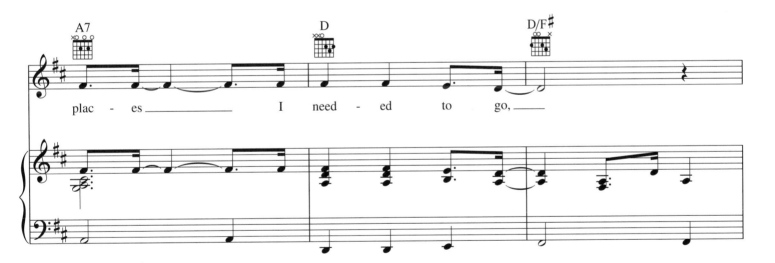

plac - es _____ I   need - ed   to   go, ___

all   of ___ the   peo - ple ___ I   need - ed   to   know. __

They knew who ___ I need - ed ___ and

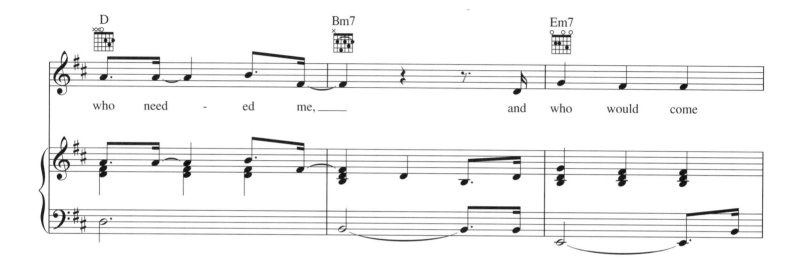

who need - ed me, ___ and who would come

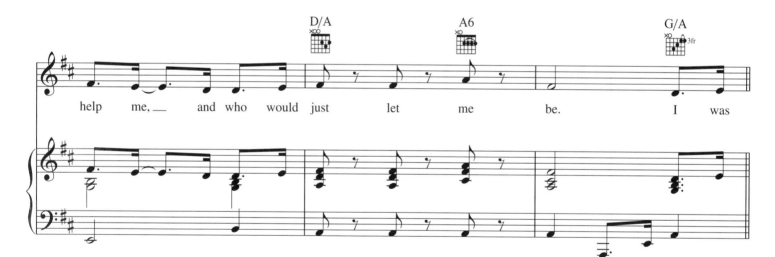

help me, ___ and who would just let me be. I was

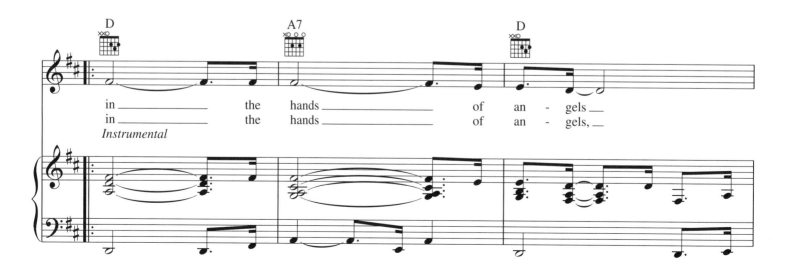

in ___ the hands ___ of an - gels ___
in ___ the hands ___ of an - gels, ___

Instrumental

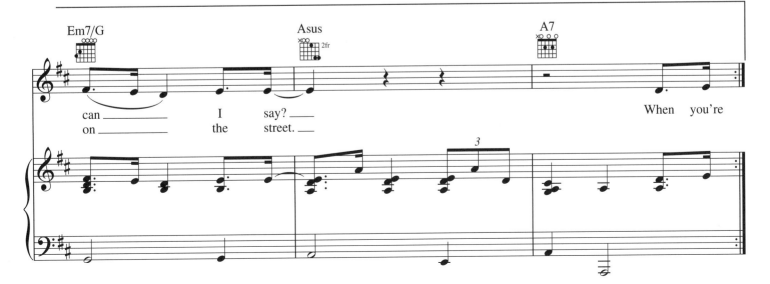

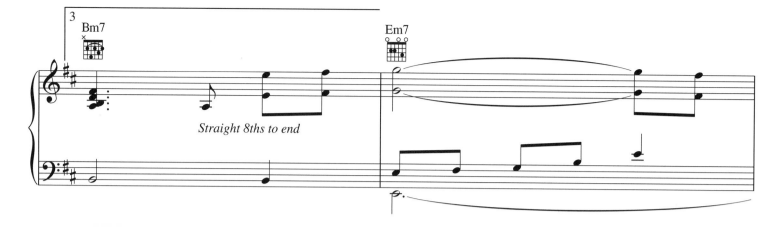

Straight 8ths to end

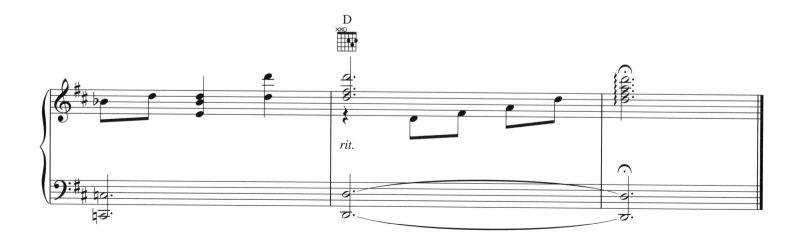

rit.